THE POWER OF PURPOSE AND PRIORITIES

LEADING THE WAY

Additional books by Leon Drennan:

People – Your Grestest Asset or Biggest Headache
Seasons of the Soul – Which one are you in?
Good King / Bad King – Which One Are You?

THE POWER OF PURPOSE AND PRIORITIES

LEADING THE WAY

LEON DRENNAN

Vision Leadership Foundation
Brentwood, TN

THE POWER OF PURPOSE AND PRIORITIES

Published by Vision Leadership Foundation, Brentwood, TN 37027
©Copyright 2016 Vision Leadership Foundation. All Rights Reserved.

Any form of duplication—physical, digital, photographic or otherwise is expressly forbidden, unless authorized in writing by the author/publisher.

ISBN 978-0-9904033-6-4

Scripture quoted in this book comes from one of the four sources noted below. Unless otherwise noted, the default verson for use is the New American Standard Bible.

Scripture taken from THE HOLY BIBLE, ENGLISH STANDARD VERSION® (ESV®) Copyright © 2001 by Crossway, a publishing ministry of Good News Publishers. Used by permission. All rights reserved.

Scripture taken from the KING JAMES VERSION, public domain.

Scripture taken from the NEW AMERICAN STANDARD BIBLE®, Copyright © 1960, 1962, 1963, 1968, 1971, 1972, 1973, 1975, 1977, 1995 by The Lockman Foundation. Used by permission.

Scripture taken from THE HOLY BIBLE, NEW INTERNATIONAL VERSION®, NIV® Copyright © 1973, 1978, 1984, 2011 by Biblica, Inc.® Used by permission. All rights reserved worldwide.

The contents of this book are based on my recollection and understanding of Scripture as inspired by the Spirit and by a lifetime of leadership experience in a large, complex organization, as well as on the observation of others in leadership roles. My thoughts have been influenced by some great books and Christian authors as referenced in this book. Any perceived similarities to leadership or management materials in the marketplace are coincidental except those which I have specifically cited. — Leon Drennan, Vision Leadership Foundation

Dedication

This book is dedicated in loving memory to my mom and dad, who taught me to work hard, persevere, and pursue God. Also, to my children Scott, Allyson, and Kelsey—in birth order. They bring me great joy and gave me three good reasons to persevere. Finally and most importantly, to my wife Debbie who has loved me unconditionally for thirty-eight years and who has persevered with me. She is my greatest single joy on this earth.

Acknowledgments

I thank Diana Rush, my executive assistant of many years and trusted friend, who worked a full-time job and helped in her spare time with formatting in this book. Finally, I thank all my past colleagues, employees, peers, and associates for the fun we had together, what I learned from them, what we accomplished together, and, most importantly, for their friendship. Also, a big thank you to Scott Drennan and Darrel Girardier for their inspiring work and design of the book cover. A special thanks goes to Fred MacKrell at AuthorTrack.com, who guided me in every major phase of this project. Thanks also for adding his creativity to the graphics and layout of the book.

THE POWER OF PURPOSE AND PRIORITIES

Table of Contents

Preface		ix
Introduction		xi
Part I	**Purpose**	1
Chapter 1	Purpose	3
Chapter 2	Confusion and Diffusion	11
Chapter 3	How Do You Execute Purpose in Your Organization	19
Chapter 4	The Cathedral	31
Chapter 5	What Is Your Purpose As a Leader	37
Part I	**Priorities**	45
Chapter 6	Less Is More	47
Chapter 7	A Priority Driven Life Requires Pruning, Balance, and Focus	61
Chapter 8	Helping People Balance Their Priorities	73
Chapter 9	Spiritual Priorities	79
Chapter 10	Conclusion	85
	Endnotes	87

THE POWER OF PURPOSE AND PRIORITIES

Notes

Preface

I've always been fascinated with people, leadership, and organizations. I learned about these growing up on the family farm, hauling hay as a teenager, working in a factory, working in a rock quarry in my college years, spending thirty-five years in business, church, and non-profit organizations, and through studying the leadership of kings in the Old Testament.

I realized as a young man that my calling and passion was to develop leaders and help improve organizations. I worked for thirty-one years at Hospital Corporation of America (HCA), the largest for-profit hospital company in the world. I was blessed with the opportunity to lead in a variety of executive roles.

My calling and passion never changed though I wore many different hats and worked with people in many different professions in my career. I loved developing people and building, redefining, and improving organizations.

Although my division was maturing and growing fast, I began to sense God leading me to make a move. I swallowed hard and, in faith, started making plans to leave the company where I had spent most of my adult life. It was one of the hardest things I've ever done.

I formed a nonprofit organization—Vision Leadership Foundation—where my goal is to train, coach, and mentor leaders using what God has taught me through many years and varied experiences. This phase of life involves developing leaders and helping organizations function better in the business, non-profit, and ministry sectors. The goal is to help leaders:

- Lead using spiritual principles and practical wisdom.

- Get more done in less time and with less frustration and stress.

- Have more time for their spouses, children, churches, communities, friends, and enjoyment of life.

- Create healthy organizational cultures to benefit their employees rather than bring difficulty and stress into their lives.

- Create more profitability, if they are business owners, so they have more financial resources to contribute to ministries and charities.

My prayer is that you will learn more quickly what it took me more than thirty-five years to figure out about the power of purpose and priorities. Doing so will give you more time to be a better spouse, parent, church member, and civic leader.

Introduction

Everywhere I go, I see people in a hurry and frustrated. The best word I can use to describe them is frenzied. And the problem is getting worse. Why is this occurring? There are two important reasons. One is they don't know why they do what they do. They don't understand their purpose. The other is that they don't have a sense of focus or priorities. They treat too many things as equally important. They are trying to do too much. They are not accomplishing all they would like to. Their energy is drained. Their frustration builds. They intuitively know something is wrong but don't know how to fix it. Less than 5% of the people I know have a clue about their purpose or mission in life. It's not even something that most people think about deeply. And they suffer the consequences of not answering this all-important issue.

One consequence is unclear or changing priorities. How do you set clear, consistent, and meaningful priorities if you're not clear about your purpose in life? Equally important is that if you're not clear about your purpose, you will not have the endurance to overcome obstacles and persevere to significant accomplishments.

Priorities separate the really important from the rest of your activities. When the really important ones are completed, you have a sense of accomplishment because you know something that mattered got done. When you know what God put you on this earth to do, then you can discern what your priorities need to be. Without this, you tend to chase the urgent, do what's easy first, or simply please the people around you.

Purpose not only helps clarify priorities, but it helps us accomplish our priorities. Usually, important things take longer and are harder to accomplish than the other things on our to-do list. When you're trying to accomplish important and difficult things with your life, you need stamina and endurance. What is it that gives you this endurance? The ultimate example is Jesus. He said, "I came not to be served but to serve and give my life is a ransom for many." It was His understanding of His purpose for being on this earth, coupled with love, that led him to endure many struggles, incredible suffering, and finally death.

When you're clear about your purpose, it helps you to define your priorities. When you focus on priorities, you accomplish important, meaningful things that give you a sense of contentment and fulfillment. When you focus on priorities, you accomplish much more with your time and your life. You're not as hurried, stressed, or frenzied. You have endurance to do the hard work to complete your priorities. Without this, you will tend to simply give up.

Examples

First, there is the apostle Paul. In his early years, he didn't know his real purpose for being on earth. He worked himself into a frenzy keeping all sorts of religious rules. He also spent a great deal of time going from city to city persecuting Christians. Once he got clear about his real purpose of being a missionary, the results were extraordinary. He wrote a great deal of the New Testament—much of it out of a prison cell. He evangelized much of the known world at the time. And he endured well beyond what most people are capable of. See what Scripture says about him.

Five times I received from the Jews the forty lashes minus one. Three times I was beaten with rods, once I was pelted with stones, three times I was shipwrecked. I spent a night and a day in the open sea. I have been constantly on the move. I have been in danger from rivers, in danger from bandits,

in danger from my fellow Jews, in danger from Gentiles;
in danger in the city, in danger in the country,
in danger at sea; and in danger from false believers.
I have labored and toiled and have often gone without sleep;
I have known hunger and thirst and have often gone without food;
I have been cold and naked. Besides everything else,
I face daily the pressure of my concern for all the churches.
Who is weak, and I do not feel weak?
Who is led into sin, and I do not inwardly burn?
2 Corinthians 11:24-29 (NIV)

Another example is the apostle Peter. Initially, he lacked focus and discipline, letting a servant girl intimidate him when Jesus was arrested.

Now Peter was sitting outside in the courtyard,
and a servant-girl came to him and said,
"You too were with Jesus the Galilean."
But he denied it before them all, saying,
"I do not know what you are talking about."
When he had gone out to the gateway,
another servant-girl saw him
and said to those who were there,
"This man was with Jesus of Nazareth."
Matthew 26:69-71

He denied three times the man he once said he was willing to die for (cf. Matthew 26:33).

But once he discovered his purpose—being an apostle to the Jewish people—and was filled with God's Spirit, he had incredible endurance and results. The man who previously was intimidated by a servant girl ultimately was willing to be crucified upside down.

THE POWER OF PURPOSE AND PRIORITIES

Then there is the ultimate example, Jesus. Scripture says:

> *For even the Son of Man did not come to be served, but to serve, and to give his life a ransom for many.*
>
> *Mark 10:45*

Because He was so clear about His purpose and the mission He was to accomplish, He often went against the conventional wisdom of the day and the advice of His disciples to stay rigidly focused on his priorities. He accomplished more in three years than others accomplished in a lifetime. And, He endured to His death. Not just any death, but death by crucifixion.

Since purpose is the key to setting priorities, we will deal with it first. Initially, we will talk from a personal perspective. Then, since life is lived out for most of us in organizations, we will look at purpose from an organizational perspective and examine the impact leaders have on people through organizations.

Part I

Purpose

"For you have been called for this purpose..."
1 Peter 2:21

*"Your eyes have seen my unformed substance;
and in your book were written all the days that were
dreamed for me, when is yet there was not one of them."*
Psalm 139:16

Questions

- Do you have a clear sense of why God has placed you where you are? The job you are in? The family you belong to? The place where you live?

- Are you clear about the purpose He created you to serve in this world?

THE POWER OF PURPOSE AND PRIORITIES

Notes

Chapter 1

PURPOSE

> Thought:
> Have you asked yourself the age-old questions:
> "Who am I? Why am I here? Where do I fit? Why does it matter?"
> —Chuck Swindoll

"Where there is no vision, the people perish."
Proverbs 29:18 (KJV)

Everyone has his own vocation or mission in life; everyone must carry out a concrete assignment that demands fulfillment. Therein he cannot be replaced, nor can his life be repeated, thus everyone's task is as unique as is his specific opportunity to implement it. [1]

– Victor E. Frankl

The Power of Purpose and Priorities

Dad

I saw the importance of purpose first in my dad's life. I was just a kid the first time I ever saw Daddy cry. Dad was a dairy farmer. He was emotionally and physically tough. I had seen him cut himself with a chainsaw and only flinch. I had seen the flesh on his hand gape open to the bone. But I had never seen him cry. One day he slipped and broke his foot. He couldn't go to the barn and milk his cows for about two weeks. I'll never forget seeing him sitting on the couch crying. It wasn't the pain of the broken foot. As he sobbed he said, "I'm just no good for anything."

Of course that wasn't true. He was a dad, a husband, and fulfilled many roles in life other than farming. But, like most people, he linked much of his self-worth and purpose to his work. When he couldn't work, he did not feel he was achieving his purpose. Dad made the same mistake that I and many others make. He associated his identity and value more with the work he did than anything else.

Life on the farm

I didn't like being out in the cold in the winter. But there were many things I did like about growing up on a farm. I could look behind the tractor after I plowed a field and see what I had accomplished. I could look at the milk can and see the milk after I milked the cow. I could see a full barn after I hauled hay all day.

I knew the purpose of plowing the field, milking the cow, and hauling the hay. And I felt a connection to that purpose and a sense of accomplishment. I felt like what I did counted—that I mattered that day.

Contrast that to work in organizational life. It's so easy to work a day or even a week and often feel like you're further behind than when you started. That zaps a person's energy and zeal for the job. That's because people need to feel like they're contributing to some purpose that matters. If we cannot see how we contribute, we don't feel like we matter. To be optimistic and highly productive, people need a clear vision of a better future and how they impact it meaningfully.

Chapter 1 – Purpose

Working in an effective organization is like time on the farm. At the end of the day, week, or year, you accomplish something, know the purpose for it, and feel a strong connection to that purpose. When the individual's purpose is aligned with the organization's purpose, there is very high morale and low turnover. Working in a weak organization feels the opposite—no feeling of accomplishment, purpose, or connection to what matters.

Professional Life

"I want to make a difference." That's the desire I've heard expressed most frequently in thirty-five years of my professional career. There are many ways people say it, but it all means the same thing. They want to matter—to have meaning and purpose. They say it in organizational meetings, in annual reviews, and in everyday life in the hallways. I've literally heard it hundreds of times.

> **Purpose is to people's souls like oxygen is to their lungs.**

Mark and Janine

I saw Mark a few months ago. He was really tired. After he told me about his schedule, I understood why. He was putting in a lot of hours and hard work. I was curious as to why he didn't do something else. He was very qualified and can make a good living with other companies without the long hours and intense schedules. I asked him why he was doing this and learned he was setting the pace and putting the expectations on himself. The company wasn't demanding long hours. The reason he was working so hard was because he saw a window of opportunity to really make a difference in the lives of people through his project. He believed it would improve the quality of health care for patients and make a difference for the company. When the discussion was over, it all boiled down to one thing. He genuinely wanted to make a difference.

I'm also reminded of Janine. She's not a high-level executive in a health care company like Mark. She is a lower-level employee with a company that helps dry out buildings after floods or any kind of water damage. She came to my house on the Saturday following the great flood of Nashville in May 2010 when she was supposed to have the day off. She had worked two weeks without taking even a day off. I had some flooding in the basement, and she remembered something that she wanted to check. She came to my house not for the money, not to further a career, and not for the recognition. She came because she cared about people and their lives and wanted to make a difference. And sure enough, she found an area of mold, which had been overlooked. She did make a difference!

Retirement

I remember vividly how I felt the first year after I retired from HCA in 2010. I created my nonprofit foundation—Vision Leadership. I thought I would immediately be busy training and coaching leaders. Yet I did almost nothing in this area for the first year. I was confused and frustrated. I did not understand God's purpose in that first year. It was for rest and reflection and to think deeply about what I really believed and understood about leadership. It let me clear my head and prepared me to write my first book, *Good King/Bad King*.

During my confusion, I had no feeling of meaning or purpose. I was absolutely miserable during this season. An existence where you don't think you matter is a small taste of Hell. I now understood why my dad cried when he couldn't milk the cows. I could also relate to my friend who retired from being the CEO of a large company. I asked him if he was enjoying retirement. His words were, "it doesn't feel good to feel irrelevant."

We all need to feel like we matter. As I do executive coaching with organizations and meet the frontline people, their most frequent and significant complaint is that the leadership doesn't make them feel valued. Everyone needs to feel they matter and know why.

Chapter 1 – Purpose

Where does this need for purpose come from?

There are numerous articles available on the subject, and the issue is raised in some secular seminars. None of these secular sources, however, deal with where the need comes from and why it exists. The best answers are in the Bible. Chuck Swindoll says it well in *Living the Psalms*: "All of us need to be needed. We want to be wanted. God created us with the desire to know we can contribute something valuable and have a significant impact on the lives of others. In years past, great men and women wanted to leave their mark on the world, to create a legacy that would continue after they passed away."[2]

Your unique purpose

"God has a purpose for each life he creates, and the purpose is as unique as the individual's fingerprint." Unfortunately "some people seem to drift aimlessly through life, with no specific direction."[3] Scripture says:

> *"Your eyes have seen my unformed substance;*
> *and in your book were written all the days*
> *that were dreamed for me,*
> *when as yet there was not one of them."*
>
> *Psalm 139:16*
>
> *"For you have been called for this purpose..."*
>
> *1 Peter 2:21*

God had a plan for your life before He ever created anything. His plan for you is a good plan (Jeremiah 29:11). It's a unique plan, created especially for you. Nobody else ever has been or ever will be created to occupy your specific time, place, and plan in the course of human history. As Psalm 139:16 says, "God knew every detail of our lives before He made us. God designs our days to form us into the kind of person He wants us to be."[4]

The question before each of us is whether we will discover His plan for us, which is best because of His infinite wisdom and love, or create and follow our own plan. "God has a purpose for each life He creates, and each purpose is as unique as the individual's fingerprint."[5]

What's that got to do with life in corporate America, churches, ministries, and nonprofit organizations? I've seen enough discouragement in all these types of organizations to be convinced people are slowly dying emotionally and physically from their perceived lack of impact. It's just so slow and common that it's not viewed as a problem. People work really hard without clear direction and purpose. They don't have a clear understanding of what God designed them to do in this world, how what they do has a meaningful impact on the organization or the betterment of other people.

Meaningful Work

I remember a study about meaningful work. The going rate for ditch diggers was $10 per hour at the time. People were hired and paid $12 per hour. Needless to say, this attracted a lot of attention. The first day, they dug a ditch and were paid. The next day, they filled in the ditch and were paid again. This was the routine. Dig a ditch one day and fill it in the next for $12 per hour. After a few days, the workers began to lose interest. Half the workforce quit. They raised the pay to $15 an hour, 50% above the market rate for ditch diggers. After a few days of the same routine, half that workforce left. This continued until the pay for digging and filling in a ditch was $25 per hour, two and half times the going rate. Finally, no one was willing to work even at this rate. Why? When the workers were interviewed, they said the extra money wasn't worth it because they lost all sense of meaning in their work. Digging a ditch only to fill it in again served no useful purpose. And the workers weren't willing to do it.

I do not agree with the nihilist philosopher Friedrich Nietzsche about some things, but he got it right when he said, "A man can bear any what if he has a big enough why."[6] The why Nietzsche refers to is meaning or purpose in life. Purpose matters! I have seen firsthand in business and ministries that people will give their lives to achieve a meaningful purpose.

Some are willing to die for a great cause. People are willing to work only so hard in a job, but they will give their all for a great purpose.

> *We are never really happy unless, and until, we are moving toward the accomplishment of something that is important to us.*[7]
>
> —*Brian Tracy*

Notes

Chapter 2

CONFUSION AND DIFFUSION

> Thought:
> How much of your time and energy is being diffused by you by your confusion about your purpose and calling in life?

"You have been called for this purpose..."
1 Peter 2:21

There seems to be a great deal of confusion about the issue of work, spirituality, and purpose in our lives. Some people have not thought a great deal about it and find the topic interesting and challenging. Others are confused and, frankly, clueless about the issue. Perhaps the most common form of confusion is compartmentalization of spiritual life, work life, and the rest of life.

Many people think spiritual work is done only in churches or ministries. They work very hard at their jobs and then spend a great deal of time in church programs and other ministries to feel good about their service to God. Sadly, they don't understand that God intended for them to find purpose in their work and view it as a spiritual act.

> *"The master in the art of living makes little distinction between his work and his play, his labor and his leisure, his mind and his body, his information and his recreation, his love and his religion. He hardly knows which is which. He simply pursues his vision of excellence at whatever he does, leaving others to decide whether he is working or playing. To him he is always doing both."* [8]
>
> — *James Michener*

Is this how you feel about your work? It's certainly not for most people I know. Why is that? The first reason is that we live in a fallen world. The second and most important reason is that the enemy of our souls tells us lies through our culture that we have come to believe. Let's look at some of those lies.

Lie # 1 — Our work is not spiritual

When God put Adam and Eve in the Garden of Eden, there was no church or ministry. There was only the work He gave them to do as a gift to them. Their work in caring for His creation was their service to Him and an expression of their worship. Our work likewise has purpose, is spiritual, and should be done unto God and not men. Jesus worked as a carpenter many more years than He worked in ministry. Martin Luther said it well: God milks the cows through the milkmaid.

God, who is Spirit, worked. His work is expressed in creation. First, He created form and structure from nothing. Then He caused His creation to flourish. He created man in His own image. This means we are like God, we work to bring order to God's world, and we use our talents and passions to honor God. We do this through our work.

Lie # 2 — Our work determines our worth

The first thing most men ask each other is, "What do you do"? We tend to value people based on their jobs, incomes, power, and status. Yet James 2:1-13 says favoring rich people over poor people is inconsistent with a profession of faith in Christ. When we understand Christ offered His life for us just as we are, we realize we have value as human beings regardless of what we do. Often, we know this truth but struggle with needing to feel productive to feel of value.

If you have children, think about this with me. When they were babies, did you love them more than you thought was possible? Of course! Could they do anything for you? No. Did you have to do nearly everything for them? Yes! Did they do anything to earn your love? No. Did you love just being with them and holding them and looking at them? Of course. When they got older and could do things for themselves, did you miss those earlier years when they were more dependent on you and you had to do more for them? I did. My children can make me proud and they do regularly. They can disappoint me and have done so on a few occasions. But even when I'm disappointed, I don't love them any less and I certainly don't value them any less as my children. They have immeasurable value to me whether they do anything for me or not.

As parents, we know and accept these things. We just have a hard time accepting that God loves us infinitely more than we love our own children.

Lie # 3 — Our work determines our identity

This lie sets a trap. If this is the case, what happens when we leave our jobs? When I left HCA to form a nonprofit organization, I left substantial income, status, and organizational power and consequently struggled with feeling like I had lost my identity. Even though I knew it was a lie from Satan, I struggled. If we find our identity in anything other than our relationship with Jesus, we can easily be manipulated by others, the world around us, and the enemy of our soul.

Work is a means to honor God and carry out His purpose for our lives. But it does not define us. Since we are created in God's image and are to carry on the work in creation that He started, we are to do our work to bring glory to God. If we see our work expressing whom God created us to be using the gifts and talents He gave us, then God should get the glory for our work. After all, we are simply expressing what He created us to be using the talents and gifts He gave us.

If our work becomes our identity, we will always seek the honor for ourselves. This will cause us to be selfish, insecure, and fearful. After all, if something happens to our jobs, we become nobodies in our own minds unless we can get new jobs.

Lie #4 — Work is a necessary evil

In Genesis, God worked. Genesis 2 shows that God works not only to create, but also to care for His creation. God worked for the sheer joy of it.[9]

When we understand the early chapters of Genesis, we see that work was part of paradise.[10] If you subscribe to the view that work is a necessary evil, there are significant implications. For one, you will believe the only good work is that which helps to make money so we can support our families and pay others to do the tasks we consider menial.[11]

Another implication is that we believe lower paying work is an assault on our dignity. A tragic result of this belief is that many people pursue jobs they're not suited for. They choose careers that do not fit their personalities, gifts, or callings for bigger paychecks and more status.[12]

Another negative result is that people choose to be unemployed rather than work at jobs they believe are beneath them. Many people believe service and manual labor jobs fall into this category.

The truth is we need to work. We were created with that need. If you were to ask people in nursing homes or hospitals how they're doing, you would often hear that they wish they had something to do, some way to be useful to others.[13]

Dorothy Sayers said work is not primarily something one does to live, but the thing one lives to do. It is, or at least should be, the full expression of the worker's faculties and the medium in which he offers himself to God.[14]

Lie #5 — The Christian leader's only spiritual duty in the workplace is to evangelize

While evangelism is good, the gospel requires far more. As King David realized in 2 Samuel 5:12, he was blessed with a leadership position so he could bless the people around him. Just as God created form and matter out of nothing then caused His creation to flourish, good leaders bring structure and order to their organizations then help people in them and those touched by them to flourish. They create an environment where people can use their passions and gifts to impact society for good. Mother Teresa once said, "Tell other people what Jesus is like, speak if you must." The godly leader blesses people and causes them to wonder why. This provides an entree to speak about their faith.

Lie # 6 — Only people in ministry have a calling

Martin Luther was adamant that all work, even secular work, was as much a calling from God as the work of a monk or priest.[15] Lutheran theology rightly stressed the dignity of work. It taught that God cared for, fed, and clothed children and supported the human race through our labor. When we work, Luther said, we are the fingers of God and the agents of His love and care for others. [16]

Practicing God's Presence

When we understand God's purpose and calling, we have a new perspective that gives our lives direction, focus, energy, and endurance. The greater our purpose, the greater our power for accomplishing great things in simple ways.

A case in point is Nicolas Herman, who was born in France during the 1600s. He was seriously injured in a military battle at an early age and became an assistant for a local government official. Desiring a richer spiritual life, he joined a monastery when he was 50 years old and was assigned to the kitchen, which he took as an insult. He did his work dutifully but had a grudge and found no joy in it. Then he decided to change his thinking. He realized that any work done for God's glory was holy. His attitude and demeanor changed over time. He began experiencing joy, which others noticed. They began asking him the reason for his joy given his role. He told them and they began seeking his counsel. One man was especially impressed and inquired about Nickolas's walk with the Lord. He made notes of the conversations, and used them to write *The Practice of the Presence of God,* which was published in the mid-1600s and attributed to Brother Lawrence, the name Nicholas went by in the monastery. Think about the impact Nicholas had through seeing the purpose in a menial task and doing it with joy to serve the Lord.[17]

Chapter 2 – Confusion and Diffusion

Application

What is the relationship of your work to your purpose in life and your calling?

_____
_____
_____

Do you believe your work is a spiritual service?

_____
_____
_____

Do you work to be in charge or to serve people?

_____
_____
_____

In what ways are you letting your work define your worth and identity? How will you correct this?

_____
_____
_____

THE POWER OF PURPOSE AND PRIORITIES

Do you know the purpose for your life? What is it?

_____
_____
_____

How do you help the people around you know they matter?

_____
_____
_____

Chapter 3

HOW DO YOU EXECUTE PURPOSE IN YOUR ORGANIZATION?

> **Thought:**
> How much easier would it be to lead and guide your organization if everyone agreed with the mission and were excited about the vision? Do your people even know the mission and vision of your organization?

"Come, let us build the wall of Jerusalem..."
Nehemiah 2:17 (ESV)

THE POWER OF PURPOSE AND PRIORITIES

People need to feel connected to a purpose larger than themselves. Hire people who are mission driven. This is why Steve Jobs was so successful.[18] That's one of many reasons so many people wanted to work for HCA. They felt they were part of something really significant. The leader needs to help people see their purpose in the organization. People need to understand where they fit in and how they impact the organization. They also want to know where the organization is going. The most common question I was asked in interviews and organizational meetings was "Where are we going?"—though the words people used to express that idea varied.

> *"Truly great organizations are crystal clear about where they are going."* [19]

How do you know if the purpose—mission—of your organization is clear? How do you know if you've done enough to connect people to the organization's mission and vision?

Each time I think of this, I'm reminded of Jim Collins' analogy of having the right people in the right seats on the bus. If that's important, having people on the right bus is even more critical. Bill Hybels, Pastor of Willow Creek Church in suburban Chicago, says, "If your vision is not clear enough to upset some people, it's not clear enough." Sometimes, organizations act as if it's more important to have a seat filled than to have the right people on the right bus in the right seats. I've seen this many times.

Let's consider the analogy of traveling. What gives you a sense of confidence that you're getting on the right plane, subway, or bus? For me, it's really good signs! I was in London over thirty years ago on a business trip and was on the public transit system wanting to see a particular portion of the city. I had a great time with the team that day and saw good portions of London. But I never saw the portion I started out to see. One reason may have been because I was a country boy fairly fresh off the farm. But maybe one reason was the signage. After all, there were smart people with me that were just as lost as I was. That's the key, isn't it? Whether we are at the airport, subway, or bus station, we need clear signs to know where we're going. It's not a pleasant trip if we get lost along the way.

Consider this hypothetical example: Assume you go to the Nashville bus station and one line runs to Memphis while the other runs to Chattanooga. What if the signs are confusing and you, a Chattanooga passenger, gets on a bus to Memphis?

An hour into the ride, you expect to start seeing mountainous terrain. Instead, it starts getting flatter. You ask questions to those around you who are trying to sleep, work, or think. You discover the bus is going to Memphis. Now you are upset.

You start complaining about going to Memphis. You start explaining why you prefer Chattanooga over Memphis. You may even go out of your way to explain why you don't like Memphis. And you keep criticizing Memphis the whole trip.

What is this like for the rest of the passengers? The four or five people sitting closest, at the very minimum, are annoyed at the distractions and the ranting. Some of the Memphis passengers start wishing they'd chosen Chattanooga based on how good it sounds. Some are confused about which city is the best to visit or do business in.

The bottom line is, by the time you get to Memphis, you are extremely upset and the four or five people sitting around you are annoyed, distracted, confused, or upset about being in Memphis.

Assume the signage was so poor that there was at least one Chattanooga passenger for every four or five Memphis passengers. In that scenario, you would have a bus full of people who didn't have a good trip.

This is what happens in many organizations. People join without a clear understanding of the organization's mission or vision. Once they find out where they're going, they are miserable and become distractions or morale barriers to the people closest to them. Get enough of those people in the organization and the morale and productivity of the whole group will be impacted.

Creating the signs?

As you do your strategic planning, there are a few things that need to be communicated clearly. Some believe setting direction is a matter of "defining the organizational mission, vision, and values."[20] I have a different view, represented by the triangle below.[21] The arrow is the "plumb line." It shows the alignment needed for the mission—purpose—of an organization to be executed and how people fit into that context.

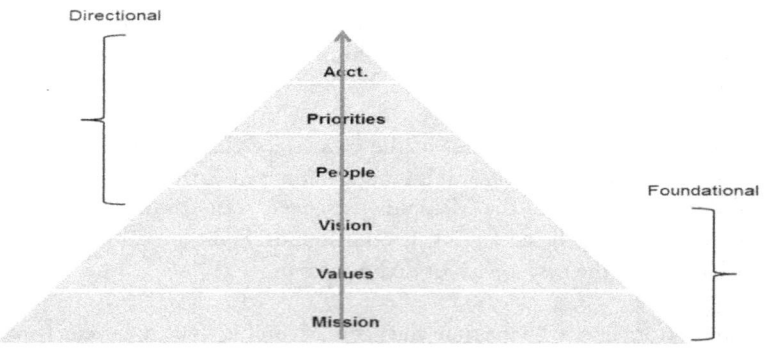

I. Mission

The mission describes why the organization exists.[22] It deals with questions like "Why are we here?" "Why do we exist?" and "Why do we get up each day and do what we do?"[23] Without mission, the organization would not receive funding, support, volunteers, or employees. Mission is about purpose, and it draws people who want to align with that purpose.[24] It is foundational to the organization. Do you know your God-given mission for your life, your career, or your organization?

The key is alignment. Everything else in the organization must be aligned with its mission or purpose. The values, vision, people, priorities, and accountability must all be aligned. Otherwise, confusion exists, efforts are diffused, and frustration builds.

In a highly effective organization, the mission represents the purpose for existence and permeates every aspect of the organization including its values, vision, people, priorities, and accountability mechanisms. It is largely pointless for an organization to spend money on teambuilding exercises and tools unless people are clearly aligned around the mission and vision.

II. Values

Our values support and must be aligned with our mission. Values clarify what you stand for and believe in.[25] Values are guiding principles that influence both "who and what fits in around here."[26] Values need to be clearly stated. But most importantly, they have to be lived out in day-to-day life by the leaders. The true values of an organization are established by the attitudes and behaviors of the leaders. To have stated values not reflected in the behavior of the leadership team is destructive and works against achieving the mission. I've seen the power of values lived out and the destructive nature of stated values not lived out. Studies have shown that people stay with organizations for less money if their values are aligned. I have seen this play out many times. People either are drawn to the values of an organization or leave because of them.

Since the mission does not change over time and the values support the mission, values are also foundational to the organization and should not change over time.

III. Vision

A vision statement is the other side of the coin of a mission statement. It is a picture of the mission fulfilled. Vision asks people to consider, "Can you imagine if...?"[27] Whereas mission speaks to the head, vision speaks to the heart to provide inspiration. Proverbs 29:13 says, "Without vision the people perish." Without vision, there is no hope for the future or sense of direction. When people lose hope, there are no goals or dreams.

While mission is a statement of what is, vision is a statement of what you would like things to be—a picture of the future you're working to create. Nothing was ever created without vision.[28]

Andy Stanley, in *Visioneering*, writes, "A vision makes you an important link between current reality and the future. Suddenly you matter. You matter a lot."[29] Remember that we said earlier it is critical for people know they matter and why.

IV. People

You hire people who care about the mission and who can do the job. If you hire qualified people who care nothing about the mission, then it is only a matter of time before they start working against the organization and in their own interests. A leader who can't or doesn't pick the right people for the organization is not a good leader. Staffing an organization with people who agree with the mission, believe in the values, are excited about the vision, understand the priorities, and accept accountability is critical to success. Employees must accept and be accountable to achieve goals that will help the organization achieve its mission and vision.

V. Priorities

Priorities help an organization focus. They should help the organization accomplish its mission. Any priorities not focused on accomplishing the mission are diluting the resources and effectiveness of the organization. Priorities save time and resources while building momentum and strength. The mission of the organization helps make the priorities clearer and more defined. When people are committed to the mission, it gives them more endurance to achieve the priorities.

VI. Accountability

The organization must have a way to hold everyone accountable for helping to achieve the mission. This should include reward and correction. Accountability is often thought of in a purely negative sense. However, biblical accountability generally is positive. Restrictions are for our benefit, and any discipline we receive is to bring us back on the right path. For example, King David said in Psalm 119:71, "It is good for me that I was afflicted, that I may learn your statutes." Scripture says those whom God loves He rebukes and chastens as a father who loves His son (Proverbs 3:11-12; Hebrews 12:3-11).

Organizational Alignment

When your organization doesn't align everything with its mission, it becomes chaotic and dysfunctional.

"Let all things be done decently and in order."
1 Corinthians 14:40 (KJV)

Our God is a God of order, not of chaos. He created something from nothing. He gave it form and structure. Then He caused it to flourish. If God gives us a leadership role in an organization, we should promote order, not of chaos. In the diagram below, purpose does not permeate the organization and the people do not flourish.

THE POWER OF PURPOSE AND PRIORITIES

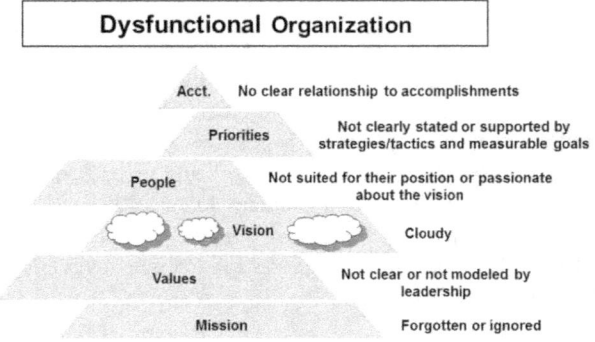

Organizations often experience **mission** creep or mission amnesia. This occurs when the organization starts operating outside the scope of its mission. Mission amnesia is when the true mission of the founder is forgotten. Harvard is a good example. It started as a seminary and has strayed from the mission of its founders. Non-profit organizations, especially churches, are at risk of mission creep. They have benevolent goals and often accomplish much through volunteers. When individuals have a good idea that helps people, they tend to take it on if they have resources to do so whether it truly fits the mission or not. If mission creep occurs, it is the first step toward organizational dysfunction. This is tragic and counterproductive because it diffuses the focus and productivity of the organization. This drift causes everything else to be affected.

Dysfunction also is created when **values** are not clear. If we don't stick with the mission, we will not likely stick with the values either. They should be written, displayed, and modeled by all leaders in the organization. The worst dysfunction occurs when documented value statements get some attention but are not modeled by the leadership. In other words, leaders don't "walk the talk."

Sometimes, leaders are so confused by the current and future environments that they don't have a clear **vision** themselves. They are trying to get past the next crisis or the next quarter. Since they don't have a clear sense of direction, they can't communicate it to their people. Some entrepreneurial founders are true visionaries, but others operate based on the idea of the day, week, month, or year.

Priorities in dysfunctional organizations often are not clear or are not supported by strategies, tactics, and measurable goals. Sometimes priorities are not aligned with the mission and vision of the organization. Sometimes people in the organization put forth new initiatives that are good ideas but not central to the organization's mission or vision. The fact that they are good, well-intended ideas and are advocated strongly by someone in the organization should not be enough for them to be pursued. If the initiatives are not critical to the organization's mission and vision, they detract attention and resources from initiatives that are critical.

Dysfunctional organizations do not have clear goals to which **people** are held accountable. This seems to be especially true for non-profit organizations. People are not aligned with the organization's mission, values, vision, or priorities.

Accountability is not clearly established in dysfunctional organizations. There is not a clear alignment of the rewards or discipline. People don't see a clear correlation between what they do and how they are recognized or disciplined financially and otherwise. Again, this seems to be particularly problematic in non-profit and government organizations. Often, people are rewarded or recognized for not rocking the boat and for their longevity in a role rather than for helping achieve specific goals. In the parable of the talents, the man who worked hard and doubled his five talents to ten was also given the talent of the bad steward who buried his one talent and did not produce anything with it.

The book *Good to Great* points out that one distinguishing feature of great organizations is their internal discipline.[30] From my experience, I believe this exists only in organizations with the right understanding of accountability. Organizations which focus too much on disciplining mistakes rather than treating them as learning opportunities create cultures of fear. Organizations that focus only on bonus programs and perks tend to create cultures where people cross boundaries chasing dollars and perks.

Summary

- <u>Mission</u> gives people a purpose.

- <u>Values</u> give them a foundation to depend on and a framework to operate within.

- <u>Vision</u> gives hope and direction.

- <u>Priorities</u> give focus and a feeling of importance.

- <u>People</u> attracted to the mission, vision, and values can be trusted with some of the priorities.

- <u>Accountability</u> gives them encouragement to do their best and course correction when they are off base.

The principles discussed in this chapter can be applied to any type of organization of any size. They can also be applied on an individual basis, especially to the leader. Just like an organization needs to be clear about its purpose and direction, individuals--especially leaders--need to be clear about theirs. If theirs are foggy, the organization is significantly affected.

Apply this to your life. Does it look functional or dysfunctional?

Chapter 3 – How Do You Execute Purpose in Your Organization

Application

Complete the following for your organization.

Mission statement:
_____
_____
_____
_____

Values statement:
_____
_____
_____
_____
_____

Vision statement:
_____
_____
_____
_____

Priorities for the next year:
_____
_____
_____
_____

Summary expectations for your leadership team:
_____
_____

THE POWER OF PURPOSE AND PRIORITIES

_____
_____

Accountability mechanisms for your leadership team:

_____
_____
_____
_____

Chapter 4

THE CATHEDRAL

> Thought:
> How much better would your organization and life as a leader be if everyone were as excited about the vision as you are?

"Whatever your hand finds to do, do it with your might."
Ecclesiastes 9:10

THE POWER OF PURPOSE AND PRIORITIES

Connecting the team to the purpose of the organization is key. People with a great purpose have great passion, energy, and resolve. This is perhaps best illustrated in the story of the cathedral.

A man noticed three bricklayers. They appeared to be doing exactly the same thing. He walked up to the first one and said, "May I ask what you are doing?" The man replied, "I am a brick layer. I lay bricks on top of each other all day long and get paid $15 an hour to feed my family. It's hard work."

The gentleman asked the second man the same question. He replied, "I'm a builder. I love building. And, it lets me feed my family."

The gentleman approached the third man with the same question. The man replied, "Oh sir, I'm building a great cathedral. I love building. But this building is special. It will be grand and beautiful. Many people will gather here to worship. Their spiritual lives and destinies will be changed in this mighty cathedral. I'm so blessed to have the opportunity to be part of this project. Can you believe it? I get to participate in something so special and actually be paid for it." [31]

All three men were performing the same activity, on the same project, and for the same pay. But they had radically different perspectives.

The first one could only see the task he performed as a duty and source of provision for his family. It felt like labor and drudgery to him. He is like those individuals in the organization who are given a task to do with no explanation of how it fits into what the organization is doing.

The second man had a broader perspective. He saw himself as a builder. He enjoyed his work and was thankful that he got paid. Unlike the first man, he was exercising his natural talents and passion in his work. He is like those individuals who enjoy being part of the organization they are with, but who are not connected mentally and emotionally to the mission and vision of the organization.

The third man saw the uniqueness of what he was building and felt truly fortunate to be part of it. He was grateful that he could be part of something so grand and, on top of that, get paid to support his family. This man was connected to the mission and vision of what he was doing. He saw the work as a privilege of being part of something bigger than himself. He is like those individuals who are committed to the mission and vision of an organization. They are using their natural talents. The mission and vision resonates with their passions. They sense they are fulfilling their destiny or calling in life. If they didn't need money to live, they would do the same thing and work just as hard at it. They illustrate the power of purpose.

Isn't this what we see in all kinds of organizations, regardless of the type of work performed? Some see their jobs as only the tasks, the labor, and the drudgery for which they get paid. Some see their work as what they do, enjoy it, and are glad they get paid. Some see their work as part of something great and feel privileged to be part of it. At times, they are amazed they get paid for doing something so wonderful.

How can organizations help their people become like the third bricklayer? It's largely up to leaders. The leader must:

- Put people in roles for which they have talent, passion, and "calling;"
- Empowering them to carry out those roles effectively;
- Support them when they need help; and
- Communicate regularly how their roles fit with the mission and vision of the organization in a meaningful way.

Example

I know a person who is a great executive assistant. She worked for a demanding executive for several years. After he left his role, I thought she would be relieved because he was so demanding and she worked so hard. After a few months, but before his position was filled, I asked her if she was happier. She said, "No, not at all." I asked her, "Aren't you working less?" She replied, "Yes." I asked, "Then, why aren't you happier?"

She said, "I did work really hard when he was here. But, he would tell me what we were doing and why. I felt like I was contributing in a meaningful way to what was happening in the company. Now I feel like I'm pushing paper, taking calls, and scheduling." In other words, she went from feeling like a cathedral builder to feeling like a bricklayer. Unfortunately, organizations do this to people frequently.

This discussion really struck me. Connecting people to the mission and vision of what we're doing changes their perspective. It's the difference between a bricklayer and a cathedral builder. Such sharing of information and perspective is something that should happen all the time in a healthy organization.

When we understand the purpose of our work, it changes our outlook. We are grateful to be part of the work. We have much greater commitment, endurance, and enjoyment in doing the work.

Application

Assess the key people in your organization. List below in three columns the ones who approach their jobs like bricklayers, builders, and cathedral builders.

Bricklayers	Builders	Cathedral Builders
_____	_____	_____
_____	_____	_____
_____	_____	_____
_____	_____	_____
_____	_____	_____
_____	_____	_____

What will you do to change the perception of those who feel like bricklayers?

_____
_____
_____
_____

THE POWER OF PURPOSE AND PRIORITIES

Chapter 5

WHAT IS YOUR PURPOSE AS A LEADER?

> **Thought:**
> If you are not clear about your purpose as a leader, how clear do you think your team will be about their purpose?

"Do not look out merely for your own interests. Look out for the interests of others."

Philippians 2:4

THE POWER OF PURPOSE AND PRIORITIES

A leader needs to answer the question, "Why am I here?" The power of leaders who know their real purpose is extraordinary. The mission, whether spoken or not, for some leaders is to exercise power, to control, to make money, and to receive perks. This doesn't match King David's understanding of leadership. Nor does it match the biblical instruction to be interested in others and not just yourself. So here's the first real question for you personally: Do you have the mindset that you are here to serve and support others? The world gives one answer and Scripture another.

Consider the example of King David. Scripture says he came to the realization God was blessing him so he could bless other people through his leadership role. David did quite well when he focused on the good of the people. It was the times he focused solely on himself that he got into trouble.

The first example is his affair with Bathsheba. Like some leaders today, he used his position for sex. Then there was the denial and cover-up when David had her husband, Uriah, killed in battle. This hasn't changed either, as some contemporary leaders use their power for cover-up as well.

Then there was the time David became prideful and had his armies counted to show how powerful he was. The result was a plague on the people. How often do leaders damage their organizations and people by pridefully focusing on what they can count rather than the difference they're making in people's lives?

In the end, David was considered a great King. God said, "He's a man after my own heart." That was because he repented, changed directions when he was wrong, and lived most of his life focused on God. But just think how much better life would have been for David, his family, and his people if his focus had stayed constantly on others.

Selfless leadership radically affects the dynamics and focus of an organization. And the outcomes are radically different than those of organizations with self-focused leaders.

Chapter 5 – What Is Your Purpose as a Leader?

Selfless Leaders

In healthy organizations, leaders are not selfish, but rather selfless.[32] They guide the team and empower it to create the best product or service for customers or constituents.

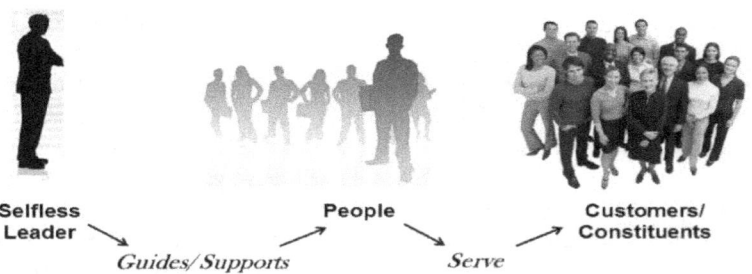

In this diagram, people and activities are focused on providing a good or service to others. Team members look to the leader for purpose, vision, and support, but their daily focus is on providing a quality product or service.

Here's a picture of an unhealthy organization.

In this organization, the leader is self-focused. Therefore, the people's first priority is determining how to please the boss rather than serving others or producing the highest quality product.

The bottom line is this: If we are self-focused, we will cause others to focus on us more than on who they're supposed to be serving. But if we serve and support our team and focus them on the mission, vision, and goal of a quality service or product, we will have a better organization.

I know people who are very servant-oriented when they go to church or take on community projects. But when they go to work, they seem to flip the switch. Rather than being servants, they see themselves as being better than others. They violate the Scripture that tells masters not to "lord it over" their people. In other words, Scripture says don't be heavy-handed with those who work for you. Yet many do not see the duplicity of being a good servant at church and in the community and being oppressive at work. I'm acquainted with some people who have great relationships in every area of their lives other than work. And it's because they see themselves differently at work than anywhere else. They see themselves as servants in other roles but not servant leaders at work. They don't realize that if they lead well and support their team well, their customers are served better, the business prospers, they prosper, and there is opportunity for their employees to prosper. Plus, the leader can receive respect and esteem from the team.

Transformation

Leaders start out with zeal and passion. We want to lead great organizations. We want to change the world. We want to grow organizations. We want to transform them into something better. We want them to be great. Many of us start with the idea that we can transform an organization without first being transformed personally, that we can grow an organization without growing personally, and that we can somehow create a great organization without improving ourselves. We want to be the fixers and the changers of organizations. We want to act like doctors to the organization that's not as healthy as it should be without being healed and fixed ourselves. Jesus told us to get the log out of our own eye before we try to get the splinter out of our brother's eye. What a great command. We would all make much better progress if we were healed ourselves before trying to fix an organization.

How would you answer these questions?

Are you clear about why God put you where you are? Are you clear about your direction in life? Are you more concerned with promoting and prospering yourself than impacting other people?

Are you clear about your values? Have you determined how you will live your life before the people you're leading? Are you going to consider other people more important than yourself? Have you come to realize that regardless of your stated values, the true values in your organization are those you live out?

Are you clear about what you expect of yourself? Are you willing to work as hard as you expect others to work? Conversely, are you willing to draw a line on the hours you work to be a good example to others? Or are you one of those leaders who will sacrifice your family for the organization? Do you expect more of yourself than you do of others?

What rewards do you seek for your leadership? Leaders who want their rewards to be primarily money, perks, and privileges will never be great leaders. Leaders who find rewards in the relationships they form, the positive impact they have on the lives of others, how much they are able to share financially with others in the organization, and how much they are able give away because of their work will be better leaders and create more productive cultures for their employees.

Since our work is part of God's plan and purpose for our lives, great leaders help people accomplish their purposes while accomplishing the organization's mission.

When you understand your purpose as a leader, you will have much greater impact on people in your organization because you will understand:

- That you are serving God by serving people under your influence;

- That you are serving a purpose beyond yourself. Leadership is difficult and we need a lofty purpose to have the energy to endure. Such a purpose gives us power to achieve what needs to be done.

Application

What about you? Is being a leader all about your power, pay, and perks? Do you have a strong sense of God-given mission and vision in your current role?

Write your personal mission statement:
_____
_____
_____
_____

Write the values you will live out in front of your people:
_____
_____
_____
_____

Write your vision of the impact your life will have over the next five years:
_____
_____
_____
_____

What are the expectations you have of yourself this year? What will you specifically do to make the team more successful?
_____
_____

Chapter 5 – What Is Your Purpose as a Leader?

_____
_____

How will you measure rewards you receive for your leadership?
_____
_____
_____
_____

Notes

Part II

Priorities

"The way is narrow that leads to life."
Matthew 7:14

Questions

- How would you like to cut your schedule of activities by 20-50% and feel like you're accomplishing more?

- Are you overwhelmed with all the activities in your life?

- Do you seem to want more out of many areas of your life, yet seem to be getting less?

- Do you know your top three priorities in life, for this week, or for today?

- Do you know your top three priorities for your job? If you don't, do you think your team can be clear about their priorities?

- Do you feel like you have enough balance in your life?

- Are your spiritual priorities clear?

Chapter 6

LESS IS MORE!

> **Thought:**
> How much time are you wasting and how much extra stress are you enduring because you're not focused on priorities?

"What has a man from all the toil and striving of heart with which he toils beneath the sun?"

Ecclesiastes 2:22

THE POWER OF PURPOSE AND PRIORITIES

In my days as a young professional, I did not understand that less in God's kingdom means more. I really believed more meant more. I tended to want it all and think if I worked hard enough, I could have it all. So I was busy all the time. In the process, I ignored my wife, kids, family, friends, and relationship with God. I gave up so much of what would have given real joy in life to chase things that, in the end, didn't matter. You don't have to do that. And you don't want to do that. You can have what Jesus referred to as the abundant life. It is wholeness in life. It is everything a person needs to experience joy and satisfaction.

Everywhere I go, it seems executives keep getting busier. There aren't enough hours in the day. The work backlogs get bigger, and the stress seems to increase. I understand. My life has felt this way many times. Let's unpack the concept of "less is more" through an illustration.

Barges, Sailboats, and Dinghies

Picture in your mind's eye a river. The river is two miles wide and is flowing at five miles per hour with barges, boats, and dinghies on it. They are spaced a safe distance apart with each carrying cargo. If you wanted to move the most goods down the river in the least amount of time, what would you do?

Let's assume you had the ability to narrow the banks of the river. Now instead of being two miles wide, it's a mile wide and flowing at ten miles per hour. For this to be safe, you have to take the sailboats and dinghies off the river, and all you have left are the barges. In this scenario, would you be able to move more goods in less time? Of course you would.

Now, let's think about any area of your life and see if this principle applies. Take work for example. Let's compare the width of the river to the breath of the project lists and activities you have. As leaders, we have many opportunities to narrow the number of activities we engage in and the number projects we pursue. Now let's compare the barges to those projects and activities that really "move the needle" organizationally[1] and the sailboats to projects that are flashy and fast but don't do much over time to advance the organization's goals. Sailboat projects often are matters of pride and have individuals' thumbprints on them—like actual sailboats often have individuals' names on them. Finally, let's compare the dinghies in organizational life to pet projects of the leader. These things do practically nothing to "move the needle," but they require resources and administrative time. By removing all "boats" from the organizational river except the "barge" projects and increasing the workflow speed, more progress can be made in a shorter period of time.

Working in a big company, I have observed many times that when the focus is narrowed to big projects that really move the needle, efficiency and effectiveness increase. We see this in the Bible in the book of Nehemiah. The great wall of Jerusalem was rebuilt in fifty-four days, a task thought unachievable. How did this happen? It was the single focus of all the people, and they did more than they thought possible during that timeframe.

Most management books have a number of tricks and techniques that are useful in helping you be more efficient with your time. But I know through experience that narrowing my focus and concentrating on high-potential projects always yields better results.

> ### *Summary*
>
> Once you have a clear purpose and the right people in place, with clear priorities and proper empowerment, then you have the chance to make real progress, but not before.

Personality profiles

Our assessment of priorities is highly dependent upon our personality profiles, how God has wired us. There are many good profile systems available, but I will explain this concept in terms of one of the oldest and simplest, the DISC profile. In this system, the D represents the dominant personality or the driver. The I personality represents the influencer or social individual. The S personality represents the steady worker. The C personality represents the cautious, compliant, and calculating individual. It's important to understand that we are all some combination of these four behavioral styles. Most of us tend to be exaggerated in a couple of areas.

The D personality tends to be a risk taker and sees opportunities. They usually envision big opportunities for the organization. The I personality sees relationships as the greatest opportunity. The S personality tends to see the work directly in front of them as most important. The C personality tends to see what can go wrong. They see the risks.

So which one is right? Here's the beauty of how God created people in this world: No single one of these is right. Rather, all are needed to get a complete perspective on what the real priorities need to be. The D personality sees the opportunity. The I personality sees the impact on people and how they must be engaged. The S personality sees the process that needs to be followed to get the work done. The C personality sees what can go wrong, providing a good risk management perspective. It's only when all these perspectives are combined and evaluated that the best priorities can be selected.

Leadership Barges

So what are the things that move the needle for a leader? This will depend on the nature of your organization and its size and scale. I will share the "needle movers" in my last organizational role. Leading the team in identifying clear priorities and breaking those into strategies and goals by department and individual took about 5%-10% of my time each year. This was one of my most critical activities because it directed everyone's focus.

Putting the right people in the right places took another 5%-10% of my time. From years of experience, I can tell you that having the right people in place is the difference between a good life for the leader and misery for both the leader and the team. As important as staffing is, I observed frequently that otherwise good leaders would get busy and not put the necessary time and focus into interviewing for and filling positions with the right people in a timely manner. There were times in turnaround situations when I literally had to make leaders give priority to people selection. They kept "putting out fires," not realizing the fires would continue burning until they got the right people in place and delegated to them appropriately.

Accountability took about 10%-15% of my time. Setting up good control systems with exception reporting and variance monitoring can take more time early on. However, once procedures are established, determining whether you are within the boundaries of what needs to be done only takes a small portion of your time.

This is the approach I used in each of my executive roles. For each area, we made sure we had good plans that everyone understood and that each individual was appropriately connected to those plans. We put the right organization chart in place and put the right people in the proper positions. Then we implemented measurement and control systems to monitor whether we were proceeding according to plan. I delegated much to capable leaders. Following this approach allowed me to do many different things without running out of time.

Priorities for Managers and Supervisors

Leaders generally have multiple managers and supervisors in their organizations. What are the priorities upon which leaders should help them focus? Let's look at what I consider the top three:

Key # 1 – Avoid a "firefighting" culture

In organizational life, everyone is trying so hard for the big breakthrough, "the grand slam," that the basics are often overlooked and problems occur, resulting in big setbacks. These setbacks require an enormous amount of time, energy, and resources to resolve. Take British Petroleum (BP), for example, and the 2010 explosion of their Deepwater Horizon oil rig in the Gulf of Mexico. According to media reports, a few more dollars spent on backup batteries and a little bit of time expended on the execution of backup routines by managers and supervisors could have saved British Petroleum $20 billion and untold stress. The list of corporate examples could go on and on.

"Firefighting" organizations never make substantial long-term progress because they focus on problems that didn't need to occur. And in their hurry to solve those problems, they tend to create their next series of problems. Avoid a firefighting culture.

During a trip to London, I decided to walk across Hyde Park back to my hotel room rather than take a taxi. I didn't know the way, so I asked someone and they said it was to the right side of the park. I headed that direction. After walking a while, I asked someone else if I was going in the right direction. They pointed me to the other side of the park. This happened about three more times. I finally got to my hotel, but I realized I had zigzagged across a five-hundred-acre park and had exerted more than twice the energy and time than would have been required had I walked in a straight line. This reminds me of organizations where priorities change frequently. They go one direction, then another, then another, wasting a lot of time and energy.

Key # 2 – Hire the right people

Jesus prayed all night before He began choosing His disciples because His decision was that important. This handful of men would change the course of human history after He was gone. One of the best ways to avoid future pain and wasted time is making sure you have the right people in place.

When I first began to lead Physician Services for HCA, there was one division out of twelve that generated 60%-80% of complaints. There was weak leadership in that division. So we went through an appropriate process to put a stronger leader in place. Within eighteen months, this division had the fewest complaints that required my attention and generated 80% of the unsolicited compliments.

That one personnel change made an amazing difference in my life as a leader. Remember, I said earlier that putting the right people in place only took 5%-10% my time, but it made a significant difference. This change was a strong example of that principle. It not only made my life better but also made life better for the hospital CEOs, the Physician Services employees, and the physicians who were employed in that division.

Putting the right people in place in an organization brings blessing and wholeness. And by the way, some people who needed to be displaced were put in other positions in the division where they could be effective. And it worked!

Key # 3 – Prioritize training and delegation

In ministry, they call this discipleship. Elsewhere, it's called training and delegation. But regardless of what you call it, it's important. Jesus knew this. He knew the rest of human history would be impacted by the few people with whom He shared His work. Jethro, the father-in-law of Moses, knew the importance of training and delegation too and gave Moses some good advice to that end. The Apostle Paul gave similar advice to Timothy:

> *"The things which you have heard from me in the presence of many witnesses, entrust these to faithful men who will be able to teach others also."*
>
> *2 Timothy 2:2*

Most leaders I know feel like they need more time, but they spend very little time training people because they don't have time. It seems to be a vicious circle. It's amazing how often leaders do work out of habit instead of thinking about who they have on the team to do the work. Leaders are reluctant to train others to do the job. Their response is, "I don't have time to train anyone." That may be true. But if you don't take time to train someone, how will you ever gain more time for yourself?

In my experience, taking time to train others in some of the tasks you do is the key to leaders' having more time and freedom. This freedom gives them time and energy to plan properly, select the right people, delegate well, and address areas of concern. These activities, in turn, produce greater progress and save more time in the future.

I know many entrepreneurial leaders who never seem to have enough time. Yet they never slow down and take the time to train people within their organizations to give themselves more flexibility and time. They seem to just keep running in circles.

Four Common Mistakes

Mistake # 1 – Unclear priorities

> *"Let all things be done decently and in order."*
> *1 Corinthians 14:40*

Teams waste enormous time and energy when priorities are not clear. I remember assuming responsibility for a new corporate department and trying to assess the priorities. It quickly became clear there was no true sense of priorities. Employees were simply trying to make the operators they were dealing with at the time happy. There was much wasted activity. Substantial money was being spent on plans and projects that had no hope of being approved. There was much other wasted activity as well with no sense of direction. Some of the activity even worked against the company in the long run.

I led the team to assess strengths, weaknesses, opportunities, and future threats. Then we put together a set of goals and priorities and had them endorsed by senior management. The team saved millions of dollars and did a better job for the company with much less stress and anxiety because they had clear priorities.

It is not uncommon in large companies for people in support areas to work really hard to make whomever they're dealing with happy but with no real sense of priority for the greater good of the organization. Non-profit organizations frequently experience mission creep. Therefore, it is common for the priorities to become blurred.

Mistake # 2 – Too many priorities

One of my group vice presidents came back from a meeting and was quite excited about the priorities the division president presented. I looked at them and quickly said, "problem." He looked at me astonished and asked what was wrong with the priorities. He asked me which ones I didn't like. I said, "Each of them is fine. The problem is there are twelve of them. Can people focus clearly on twelve different things?" My experience has shown that if you go beyond five to seven objectives/priorities for an annual cycle, you start diluting the effort and people lose focus.

> *If you have a bunch of them, they aren't all real priorities.*

So, how does focusing on priorities in your organization bless people? It creates focus. It brings simplicity out of complexity. It ensures people are pulling together toward the key priorities, resulting in greater accomplishment and satisfaction for them and the whole team. It assures the leader and employees are on the same page, resulting in fewer expectation gaps, conflicts, and instances of confusion.

> *Priorities in organizations act like river banks. Initiatives flow faster the narrower they get.*

Let's think about how a river works. The more the river banks narrow, the deeper the channel gets, and the faster and stronger the water flows. Priorities in organizations act like river banks. When you narrow the priorities, initiatives flow faster and stronger. Priorities create "tipping points" in organizations like waterfalls on a river. Things move with great speed, and a powerful, almost unstoppable, force is created.

One time I was consulting with a large church that was getting ready to double in membership. In working with the staff, I tried to assess their priorities. In a team meeting, I asked people to share their priorities. The chief administrative leader had a page of activities front and back. I said,

"I think that's too much for you to get done. What are your top three priorities?" He lifted his hands with a bewildered look and said, "I have no idea." If the lead administrative person had more than he could do and no sense of priority, what do you think that was like for the team? There was chaos, confusion, and anxiety among the team. In fact, if things proceeded, I perceived it was only a matter of time until high turnover would occur. Even though this was a church, I hardly saw it as an environment where employees were being blessed. This leader and the whole team were really good people. The church was a good church. Everybody had good intentions. People worked hard and did their best. But with a lack of clear priorities, anxiety, chaos, and confusion were rampant in the lives of these people.

Mistake # 3 – Over-controlling

God doesn't over-control us. In fact, He gives us great freedom coupled with great accountability. In our analogy of the river, the riverbanks do not micromanage each drop of water. Rather they guide the flow of the water along the path of least resistance toward the ultimate destiny of the river. When the riverbanks get too narrow, the water overflows its banks. I've seen this in an organization where overly restrictive controls were put in place. The operations people began to work around them, resulting in a complete lack of control. You can hinder your organization by over-controlling.

I am reminded of my experience on the farm with hogs and an electric fence. The hogs were shocked so many times from touching the fence that we had a very difficult time getting them to leave the hog lot even though the gate was open and there was no fence across it. When people are exposed to excessive-control environments where there are severe penalties for making mistakes, they no longer show initiative or take risk outside of what they see as the boundaries. This can have a devastating effect on an organization in the long run.

As I write this portion of the book, a national debate is occurring on government regulation of business. We are in an environment of high regulation with businesses screaming that it is causing them to be less competitive. Clearly, some regulation is needed. However, once the controlling goes too far, the costs get too high and business competitiveness and creativity is inhibited. Over-controlling becomes increasingly likely as an organization becomes larger and more bureaucratic. Also, the wrong personality profiles in key leadership positions will almost always result in over-controlling.

People want to be prudent, but they also want to be productive. They see the need for good planning and a reasonable level of control. They get really frustrated when they feel they're over-controlled and that the controls stifle productivity. Good controls give direction, protection, and create steady organizational flow. Over-control stops the flow and is counterproductive. This happens quite frequently in government and nonprofit organizations. Be careful not to apply this incorrectly when dealing with legal, health, or life and death issues where 100% is the standard.

Mistake # 4 – Favoring efficiency over effectiveness

Efficiency concerns the time and resources required to complete a project. Effectiveness relates to the value of a project and the impact it will have.
When I led the internal audit department at HCA, it was not uncommon for teams to work until eight or nine o'clock at night, have dinner, and then work more in their hotel rooms. They were incredibly efficient. Yet needless to say, we had high turnover. People left on average after six months to one year. It seemed we were always hiring, always training new people, and always trying to do complicated work with inexperienced people.

I noticed that these late nights were the norm with some supervisors while other supervisors completed their audits with more normal hours. After much discussion with the leadership team about employing efficiency techniques, we went the route of emphasizing effectiveness issues/priorities instead. Auditors like to dot every "i" and cross every "t". But not all work in an audit is of equal value. We started talking about working smarter, not harder. We prioritized the steps in each audit that were mission-critical. We never compromised on those. We held open the option of changing the scope of an audit depending on the time available. With that change, we were able to make the schedules reasonable and retain people for much longer, resulting in more qualified people doing better audit work.

I once again proved the value of emphasizing effectiveness years later when I was responsible for the Physician Services department. This was a role with substantial responsibility and a good deal of complexity. I really thought I was managing my time well and was highly focused on only the most important priorities. Then I had major surgery. I had to transition back into work first two hours a day, then four, then six, and then finally on a regular schedule. I discovered that I could do all my high-priority work in two to four hours a day. The rest of the time was spent on lesser priorities, meetings, miscellaneous administrative tasks, and bureaucratic activities that I got a "pass" on during this time. Focusing on effectiveness helped me succeed without wasted effort.

Application

I. In your organization, what activities produce most of your results; i.e., what are your barges?

_____
_____
_____
_____
_____

II. Are you zealous about protecting the time to do these activities, appropriately staffing them and funding them at a priority level?

If not, what changes will you make?

_____
_____
_____
_____
_____
_____
_____

III. Do your direct reports know the primary activities that will produce most of their results?

_____
_____
_____

THE POWER OF PURPOSE AND PRIORITIES

If not, what will you do to teach them?
_____
_____
_____
_____
_____
_____

Chapter 7

A PRIORITY DRIVEN LIFE REQUIRES PRUNING, BALANCE AND FOCUS

> **Thought:**
> Have you ever considered that your true joy, greatest impact, and progress toward your real purpose in life are being blocked by lesser goals and activities?

"I came that you might have life and have it to the full."
John 10:10 (NIV)

Different authors have similar but different ways of categorizing areas where we set goals. Dan Miller has one version; Chuck Swindoll has another. And finally, Zig Ziglar has his version. He illustrates it in this way:[33]

The Wheel of Life

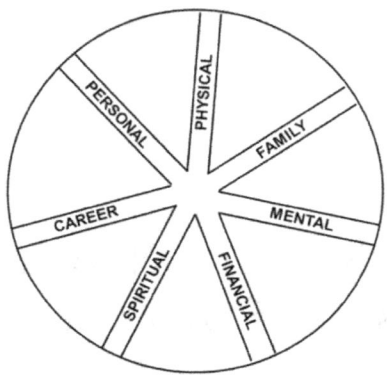

Everywhere I go, people seem busy and stressed. They are chasing what they consider the good life. They look at the various components of their lives, and they want more in each area. They truly believe that *more* is the key to happiness. Jesus said, "I've come that you have might have life and have it more abundantly." Some translations say, "I've come that you might have life and have it to the full." There's a difference between the busy and heavily scheduled life that most Americans are living and the full life that Jesus intended.

Now the question becomes, if less is more, should we just pick one or two areas of life and be highly successful in those areas? This is what many people choose to do with their finances or career.

Yet such a practice ignores other important facets of life where we must set and achieve priorities to feel whole or complete. It is true that people with a narrower set of priorities tend to achieve more in those areas, but they are not happy because they do not have the balanced life that God intended for us.

> *Henry Ford once said he didn't want executives who had to work all the time. He insisted that those who were always in a flurry of activity at their desks were not being the most productive. He wanted people who would clear their desks, prop their feet up and dream some fresh dreams. His philosophy was that only he who has the luxury of time can originate a creative thought.*
>
> *Wow! When's the last time your boss told you to quit working and do more dreaming? Unfortunately, our culture glamorizes being under time pressure. Having too much to do with too little time is a badge of "success." Or is it?* [34]
>
> —*Dan Miller blog, September 2015*

The priority driven life requires pruning

Less is more in all areas of life. I don't think you can make your life better just by being busier in any area. One counter-intuitive principle nature teaches us is that the healthiest and most robust plants require pruning. Yes, you have to cut things back—prune them—for them to reach their optimal health, growth, and beauty. Henry Cloud, in his book *Necessary Endings*, teaches us this through his illustration of pruning rose bushes.[35]

> *The most healthy, beautiful rose bushes were pruned properly.*

There are three kinds of branches that need pruning on a rosebush:

- **Dead branches that are taking up space needed for healthy ones.** Evaluate all areas of your life. What activities are dead—those that bring you no joy, give you no feeling of purpose, and are not necessarily helping anyone else? You do these out of habit or obligation. Cut these out.

- **Sick branches that aren't going to get well.** These activities aren't totally useless, but they don't bring real joy or meaning. And that's not going to change. Cut these out.

- **Healthy branches that aren't the best.** My pastor, Mike Glenn, says, "Good is the enemy of best." There are activities in your life that are good. They bring you joy, help other people, and you see purpose in them. Yet they take time that could be spent on even more purposeful activities with more impact for you and others. Cut them out to allow time for the best.

Let's look at several key areas of life and think about pruning that needs to be done in each area.

Career

Most people I know have jobs with too many projects. Isn't that what we face in our jobs? We have more projects than time. Our choices are to decide which projects we are not going to do so that we can spend our time and do the projects that "move the needle" well, or we can spread limited time among all projects and risk doing all of them poorly, resulting in failure.

We accomplish more over time by choosing a few high-priority projects and doing them well rather than spreading limited time among too many projects. In doing this, we prove that "less is more" because we accomplish more in the long run. Also, we experience less stress and frustration because we are not stretched too thin. We aren't stressed over giving inadequate time to important projects.

There was a time I had flu-like symptoms and could not work a normal schedule for about two weeks. I thought I was being a very good time manager. But when I looked at my schedule and eliminated everything that was not mission-critical, I was able to cut my schedule in half. **Less is more on the job!**

Family

Everywhere I go, I see families busy and worn out, especially the mom and dad. Many parents I know feel like taxicab drivers. They're always taking kids from one event to the next. They eat fast food and seldom have time for a meal around the table. Many are talking at, not with, their kids. Most people I know with children work really hard at having a good family life, but almost none are really content with the family life they have. Why? They're trying to do too much. They think that more is more. If they scheduled fewer activities and put more time into meaningful activities together with a purpose, their family life would be better.

My kids almost never talk about all the ballgames and other activities on which we spent so much time and energy. They talk about occasions when we spent a block of time as a family doing something special together or helping someone. Being busy all the time didn't make family life better. **Less is more in family life!**

My kids taught me good lessons in this area. One time, my son called wanting me to do something. I thought I was being responsive and efficient by taking care of what he needed and sending a message back through my executive assistant. She came to me and said, "Scott is demanding to talk to you." I picked up the phone and he "lit into me." He said, "I am your son. I get to talk to you!" He reminded me of a very important principle: Sons and daughters have special privileges. As sons and daughters of God, we have special privileges. We are always welcomed at the throne of grace because we often need it. Having genuine communication is really important in family life.

I had a similar incident with my daughter Allyson. She asked me for some help. I did everything she asked and more. But I sent the message back through my assistant. She got very upset, thinking I had ignored her.

My rule became that if my kids ever called, it didn't matter what I was doing. I wanted to be reached, and I wanted to talk to them. Kids want and need the undivided attention of their parents more than they need all the activities on which we spend so much time.

Church life

Most churches I know are brimming with programs. There are activities seven days a week. They are all well intentioned. Many are good, and some are excellent. Yet the activities of many churches need to be pruned. Some of the activities and programs are truly dead. They have no impact. They are continued because they have strong advocates or simply because it is hard to eliminate any program in a church. Other programs are anemic. They are never going to be robust and should be cut. Some programs or activities are good but still not the highest and best use of time and resources. They should be cut to focus all the time and energy on achieving the church's true purpose. I'm convinced less would have more impact for the church.

It's particularly easy for people in ministry to consider their jobs such an overarching priority that they sacrifice health and family. It is common for people in ministry to burn out after a few years. One of the reasons is they put so much focus on their jobs that they have no balance in the other areas of their lives. They try for a while to do it all but can't and burn out. Often, they sacrifice their own families while trying to minister to other people's families.

In our own spiritual lives, we are so busy with activity that we often don't experience the depth God has for us. The Bible says, "Be still and know that I am God." We are an active people. I've seen in the lives of others and experienced in my own life that less activity often creates more spiritual growth. Less really is more.

In my own ministry activities, I've noticed that less is more. I'm a very active person, and left to my own devices would tend to fill up my calendar. God has shown me that a less busy schedule can have a greater impact. For example, Bill invited me to lunch to talk about raising children. Bill worked sixty to eighty hours a week as a consultant and routinely charged twenty hours a week less than he worked. He also charged a rate less than half of his true value. He explained he did this because he wanted to go the "extra mile." I commended him for wanting to go the "extra mile" but questioned how much of it was actually fear rather than a desire to go the extra mile. He acknowledged a great deal of it was fear. Then we talked about stewardship. I asked how much good could be done if he charged at or near market rate and charged for most of his time rather than twenty hours per week less. He had not thought of it that way.

He was considering going to a smaller church where his kids could get involved in hands-on activity. I asked what difference it would make if he charged for most of his hours at a fair rate, worked fewer hours, and took his children to a third-world country on a mission project to see how the rest of the world lives and minister to children in poverty. The lights came on for him.

I spent an hour lunch with Bill and a few hours since. He is positioning himself to work fewer hours at a much higher rate, resulting in a better income for his family, more giving to ministry, and more time for his kids. He is discovering that less is more. But God is also showing me that less is more. In a handful of hours, God gave me the opportunity to impact two generations of people. That's much more impact than I would have in a typical day of being very busy. In ministry, being available at the right time is more important than being busy all the time. Jesus took time out to rest. At times, He encouraged His disciples to step aside from their busy activities and rest with Him. **Less is more in spiritual life and ministry!**

Social

People I know who seem most content and fulfilled in community work are those that pick an organization or an initiative to support. They have a much greater impact on the community. Those who try to be involved in everything seem more stressed and less fulfilled. **Less is more in community life!**

Recreation

Some people wear themselves out on their recreational activities. The people I know who get the most out of their recreation are the ones who focus on one to two hobbies or activities. They become really good at one activity or hobby, and it seems to make their life far better, but not just busier. **Less is more in recreation!**

Physical

I know people who endure aggressive training to run marathons. A lot of people make it a point to jog or exercise at least an hour a day. There is nothing wrong with this if a person enjoys it. Some do it as a simple act of discipline, thinking it's required for optimal health. Some of the latest research on exercise physiology supports the idea of "surge" training—short bursts of intense activity with rest in between. A full surge training workout takes about eighteen minutes three to four times a week. Studies have shown that a person's overall health is as good or better doing this as jogging an hour a day seven days a week. Less is more in exercise!

How many of you were taught to clean your plate as a kid? It didn't matter that you weren't hungry. You were supposed to eat it all. In fact, when I grew up, kids got complemented for eating heartily. We Americans like our food. Studies in recent years, however, have shown that people in cultures with less calorie intake actually have longer, healthier lives. Less is more in health!

Personal development

I had a friend who seemed to listen to every new seminar and read every new book that came out related to business. I told him he needed to cut back on listening to seminars and reading books. He seemed surprised and asked me why. I told him he had already studied more material that it would take him three lifetimes to implement. I suggested he narrow the focus and begin implementing principles that would be most beneficial to his life. People seem to do a lot of self-development in many areas without ever mastering anything. You would be more productive to master a topic related to your strengths, passions, calling, and purpose. Think about the impact your life could have. Less is more in personal development!

A new agricultural extension agent was placed in a big farming community. He wanted to teach some courses on agriculture and went to the most progressive farmer in the community, hoping to enroll him. The farmer declined. The agricultural extension agent was surprised and asked him why. The farmer said, "I don't need to learn anything else. I don't do as well as I know to do now." Isn't that the case with most of us in many areas of life?

Nonprofit application

Who should be the most balanced people in our society but often aren't? Who should encourage balance in people's lives but often don't? Who should reduce guilt in our lives but often add to it? Often, it is the leadership of nonprofit organizations. Because these organizations have philanthropic missions, their leaders often do not do a good job of balancing their own lives. They believe it's impossible to give too much to their mission. But it is possible. And life can get out of balance. Balance is needed in this part of our lives just like any other part.

Summary

Narrowing our priorities allows us to focus on accomplishing a few important things. Having a clear understanding of the purpose in our priorities gives us the persistence and energy to fulfill them passionately.

When we understand work as a service to God and other people rather than just the source of a paycheck or a way to advance our careers, we will have more endurance during the hard times because we know God will reward us eventually.

THE POWER OF PURPOSE AND PRIORITIES

When we understand our role in developing our children and being a spiritual leader within the family, it means everything we do has a spiritual purpose and therefore becomes more important.

When we understand our work at church as discipling people rather than supporting programs and activities, it changes what we invest our time in as well as our intensity and focus.

When we see our social life as a way to impact others, to create great community and fellowship, and to serve God, our social interaction will take on a new dimension.

When we see our recreation and physical activity as a service to God, we will look at them differently. When we see our bodies as temples of God, we will take better care of them. When we see rest, relaxation, and recreation as something God intended for us and commanded us to do, it will take on new meaning for us.

When we see purpose in our self-development, what we do and the intensity with which we do it will change.

Application

I. What do you need to cut out of your life? Look at each of these seven areas and list things you need to prune.[3]

	High Priority – Keep	Low Priority – Prune
Career		
Financial		
Family		
Spiritual		
Social		
Physical		
Personal Development		

II. Are you clear about the purpose for which you're pruning your life? Write it out below.

_____
_____
_____
_____
_____
_____

III. What are you doing that causes you to be anxious? How can you cut it out of your life?

_____
_____
_____
_____
_____
_____
_____

Chapter 8

HELPING PEOPLE BALANCE THEIR PRIORITIES

> **Thought:**
> Have you considered how much stronger your organization could be in the long term if you helped your team be more balanced?

"Do not merely look out for your own personal interests, but also for the interests of others."

Philippians 2:4

THE POWER OF PURPOSE AND PRIORITIES

People need balance

Life is like a wheel on a car. If it gets out of balance, it feels lonely and uncomfortable. Most people I know feel their lives don't have the balance they want.[36]

Sometimes, leaders think an organization can't be successful if employees are encouraged or allowed to give significant priority to other goals in life. It's been my experience that people who are very conscious of the choices they are making and feel good about the balance they have based on their "calling" in life actually contribute the most to an organization and accomplish the most in every area of life.

I remember a movie about a dogsled race. The team that took periodic rests beat the teams that kept going all the time. This is the principle of observing the Sabbath day. People can actually get more done by resting every seventh day than by continuing to work all the time.

It is sometimes surprising to see what people will give up in life to achieve a particular goal or complete a project at their job. It's not that what they're working on is unimportant. But often people make significant tradeoffs for projects they won't remember a year later. I remember almost insisting many times that employees take time off to be with sick parents or to be at some significant event for their children. These were cases where I was really convinced they would not have done it without my encouragement. I was impressed by their dedication but marveled at their lack of insight regarding the true priorities in life. I say that remembering poor decisions I made, especially early in my career. There are many times I wish I had back to make a more holistic and conscientious decision about what matters most in life.

Jesus never seemed in a hurry. He was stressed at times, but it didn't come from having too much to do and worry over not accomplishing everything on His "to do" list. His earthly ministry was three years, and on the cross He said, "It is finished." He completed all the work He was assigned to do. Yet, Jesus had balance. I'm told the checkerboard square, which is a brand symbol of the Ralston Purina Corporation, was created by the founder to show the balance in Jesus' life.

Luke 2:52 says, "And Jesus increased in wisdom and stature, and in favor with God and man." In other words, Jesus grew mentally and emotionally, physically, spiritually, and socially. Jesus had goals and spent time in the four balanced areas of life. Yet, He did so without anxiety and stress over a busy schedule.

Wisdom – *mental and emotional*

Favor with man – *social*   **Stature** – *physical and health*

Favor with God – *spiritual*

I once interviewed what appeared to be a bright, aggressive young man. I remember asking him where he wanted to be in ten years. He said he wanted to be sitting in my chair. I said that was great because I had other goals, and I wanted to be sitting in another chair by then anyway.

Later, I offered him a job, which he promptly turned down. I asked him why. He responded that he had a dog and that he could not be out of town and leave his dog that much. I told them I respected his concern for his dog, and there's nothing wrong with being that attached to a pet. I did, however, go on to explain that he had an important decision to make. I explained that he had lofty goals he would never achieve if his goal of being at home with his dog took priority. I reminded him of saying his goal was to sit in my chair in ten years. I explained that sitting in my chair or one like it would require some changes in his priorities.

People seem to struggle with striking a healthy balance. Leaders are in a position to make the struggle harder or easier for people. We can help them or hurt them in the process. If we are going to bless people, we should help them.

A priority-driven life narrows the focus

Leaders want more time, more freedom, and less stress. How is that even possible in organizational life today? The key is how you approach life. Are you going through life like a rifle bullet or like a shotgun blast? Let me explain. A rifle bullet is much smaller than the shotgun shell. It has less powder and less lead. It takes less powder because there's only one small piece of lead that leaves the barrel. It takes less powder to propel the smaller piece of lead a great distance. By contrast, a shotgun shell has much more powder and more lead. The lead is a bunch of pellets, called buckshot. They look like small BBs. They come out of the barrel of a shotgun and scatter. They hit a bigger target area since they scatter. The shooter can be less accurate with a shotgun and still hit the target. Since the buckshot scatters and is small, it doesn't go nearly as far as a rifle bullet.

This is analogous to people's lives. Some people are highly focused on a singular objective or a limited number of objectives, and they can go far. Other people's lives have so many activities that they are more like a shotgun blast. They cover a lot of territory but don't make as much progress as people who are more focused.

Jesus modeled a life that had three critical components. First, He had balance. Second, He had a clear purpose in life. And, third, He was focused on a narrower set of goals than most people believed He should pursue.

Chapter 8 – Helping People Balance Their Priorities

Application

I. Do the people on your team have a balanced life? Yes____ No____

A. If not, are you doing anything to help them find balance? Are you encouraging a lack of balance by your example or expectations of them?

B. What changes do you need to make to encourage balance for your team?

_____
_____
_____
_____
_____

II. Do you affirm people when they make hard personal choices to achieve balance in their lives, even if you feel it is a loss for you?

Yes____ No____

THE POWER OF PURPOSE AND PRIORITIES

Notes

Chapter 9

SPIRITUAL PRIORITIES

> **Thought:**
> Have you ever considered the opportunities and joy you miss or the pain you endure by not following spiritual priorities?

"But his delight is in the law of the Lord, and on his law he meditates day and night."

Psalm 1:2 (ESV)

The New Testament speaks to the tendency of people to worry about having the basics of life. Jesus said to them:

> *"Seek ye first the kingdom of God and His righteousness, and all these things will be added to you."*
> *Matthew 6:33 (KJV)*

Jesus understood the importance of right and clear priorities in life. There are Ten Commandments in the Old Testament. A lawyer once asked Jesus which was the most important commandment. He summarized all the Old Testament by saying:

> *"Love God with all your heart, soul, and mind and your neighbor as yourself."*
> *Matthew 22:37-40*

King David

Have you ever considered what it costs a person not to follow the simple commands of God? Let's look at the life of King David again. God called him "a man after His own heart." David truly lived an outstanding life by anybody's standards. But he strayed from God's commands at times.

Bathsheba

His affair with Bathsheba is an example. He wasn't putting God's kingdom first nor did he love his neighbor as himself. He was self-focused. He took what he wanted. And he had a good man killed in battle to cover up his crime. The prophet Nathan told him that he would be forgiven, but he would pay for this seven times over. We see through studying his life that this did cost him seven times over in personal and family difficulties.

Numbering his armies

David once became prideful and wanted his armies counted to show how powerful he was. He did this over the objection of the commander of his armies. He wasn't thinking about God's kingdom when he did this; he was thinking about his own. A plague struck the nation of Israel, and 63,000 people died because of David's pride.

> *"Pride goes before destruction,
> and a haughty spirit before stumbling."*
> *Proverbs 16:18*

The good thing about David was that when he strayed from the path of God's priorities, he genuinely repented and returned to God. That's why he had a long and successful impact as a king.

Personal Experiences

It's hard for me to assess objectively what I've lost by not following God's priorities. I am aware of the anxiety and pressure I feel because I didn't start on this book immediately when God told me to write it. But I can look back at some significant experiences and see what I gained from putting God first.

When I was about thirty years old and in the number two position of HCA's internal audit department, I was frustrated. My boss did not have a good relationship with some of the company leadership. It would be years before he retired, and I felt stuck. I was assistant vice president of Internal Audit, and it looked like that's all I would be for many years. I was recruited by another healthcare organization that was smaller. They offered me a 30% increase in pay, an expensive company car, a company-paid country club membership, and what seemed like a great stock option package. As

I talked to friends and advisers, all of them but one person told me it was an offer "too good to refuse".

My pastor was the only person who encouraged me to turn it down. After much prayer, I did turn it down. The reason was that when I looked at my immediate family, extended family, church service, community service, and so on, the new position would have resulted in a loss in all those areas. The only one who would benefit from this move seemed to be me. I swallowed hard and turned it down. I had a strong sense that this was what God was leading me to do.

Within nine months, the company that offered me the job was in bankruptcy, and all the senior officers were being sued. I would have been one of the senior officers if I had made the switch. Also, my boss at HCA retired, and I had the top spot in Internal Audit, which had been a serious goal of mine for a long time. Over the next few years, the compensation and stock options I got at HCA were much more than I was offered at the other company. Making God my priority and loving others more than myself led to blessing and made a deep impression on me.

A few years later, HCA was acquired through a merger, and the senior executives had an opportunity to leave with a nice financial package or stay. All of my natural intuition and business intuition said, "Take the money and run." But I sensed in my spirit God telling me to stay. So I stayed. My natural and business intuitions proved to be more right than I could have ever imagined. It was a difficult season of life for me, and many others as well.

Yet God was working in this too. Jeremiah 29:11 came to my attention many times: "I know the plans I have for you, plans to prosper you, not to harm you." I was given many opportunities to lead departments outside of Internal Audit and eventually was given the opportunity to lead Physician Services for HCA. These various leadership opportunities gave me the experience I needed to write this book and do many things to which I believe God has called me in the future.

The move to Physician Services created the opportunity for me to have an office off the main campus and a mile down the road from my church. After a season of downsizing Physician Services, I had margin in my schedule. That allowed me, with the approval of HCA's leadership, to devote a block of my time in the role of the executive pastor at my church. After that, Physician Services experienced much growth. I learned much from these experiences that are incredibly valuable today.

What I went through felt bad, looked bad, and was very confusing to me at the time. But I knew God was leading me at each stage of the journey. Looking back, I can see how clearly He was training me and positioning me for what I would be doing fifteen years later. It prepared me to create Vision Leadership Foundation to mentor, train, coach, and consult with business, nonprofit, and ministry leaders.

Application

I. Do you follow the Scriptures noted at the beginning of this chapter when you make business and personal decisions? Yes____ No____

II. Remember some times you did and make notes below on the difference it made.

_____
_____
_____
_____
_____
_____
_____

III. Recall some times you didn't and make notes on the difference it made.

_____
_____
_____
_____
_____
_____
_____

IV. What is your main spiritual priority? What effect could it have if you organized your life according to this priority?

_____
_____
_____
_____
_____

Chapter 10

Conclusion

Do you feel like you're getting nowhere even though you're working harder? Are you tired and frustrated? Have you said to yourself lately, I don't need this? Why am I even working here? Why am I volunteering at this place?

After reading this book, have you discovered your purpose—your mission in life? Are you closer to finding it?

If not, ask yourself these questions: What have people always said you do well? What do you love doing so much that you would pursue it wholeheartedly if money weren't an object and if it were not possible to fail?

If this doesn't help, think about what makes you mad, glad, or sad. Something that makes you especially glad could be a key to your purpose.

THE POWER OF PURPOSE AND PRIORITIES

Something that makes you mad or sad—maybe some injustice you have an opportunity to address—may help you become aware of your purpose as well.

Also, ask yourself these questions: Why are you working? Who are you working for? If you're working only for self-promotion, money, power, and advancement, you will not tend to find the same energy as you would in working for others or a higher cause.

If you work as unto the Lord, you will find greater purpose and energy because you realize you're working for an eternal reward.

Can your name your top three priorities for today, this week, or this year? Do you find yourself committing to things but then not having the patience or endurance to see them through? Your answers to these questions will reveal clearly if you know your purpose and have clear priorities. If not, then you might consider working with a life coach or a minister who is skilled in helping people discover their purpose or mission in life. Not all life coaches or ministers are good at this.

Remember, you have to be clear about your purpose before you can set meaningful priorities for how you spend your time in this life. But more importantly, you have to be clear about your purpose and committed to it to have the endurance to see your priorities through.

When you combine a clear understanding of your purpose with a few focused priorities, your life will have much greater impact.

Endnotes

Note #	Reference	Text Page
1	Viktor E. Frankl, 1905-1997; Austrian neurologist, psychiatrist, and Holocaust survivor; quote attributed. Available from http://www.goodreads.com/author/quotes/2782.Viktor_E_Frankl	Page 3
2	Charles R. Swindoll, *Living the Psalms* (Brentwood, TN: Worthy Publishing, 2012), page 233.	Page 7
3	Ibid, page 277.	Page 7
4	Ibid, page 277.	Page 7
5	Ibid, page 233.	Page 8
6	Brian Tracy, Maximum Achievement, (New York: Simon & Schuster, 1993), page 161.	Page 8
7	Ibid, page 139.	Page 9
8	Dan Miller, *48 Days to the Work You Love* (Nashville, TN: B&H Publishing, 2015), page 7.	Page 12
9	Timothy Keller, *Every Good Endeavor*, (New York: Dutton/Penguin Group USA, 2012), page 21. (Note: I am indebted to Rev. Keller for his insight on the godliness of work that I refer to in this section.)	Page 14
10	Ibid, page 22.	Page 14
11	Ibid, page 30.	Page 14
12	Ibid, page 35.	Page 15
13	Ibid, page 23.	Page 15
14	Ibid, page 25.	Page 15
15	Ibid, page 4.	Page 15
16	Ibid, page 1.	Page 16

17	Brother Lawrence, The Practice of the Presence God, (New York: Fleming H. Revell Company, 1895	Page 16
18	Robert Kiyosaki, *The Key to Hiring Right*, April 30, 2006. Available from Entrepreneur.com. http://www.entrepreneur.com/article/160158#	Page 20
19	*Mapping a Clear Organization Direction*, Triaxia Partners, Inc., page 1. Available from http://triaxiapartners.com/corp/strategy/articles/Mapping-Clear-Org-Figure	Page 20
20	Ibid, page 1.	Page 22
21	Google Images, Earlsbusiness.wordpress.com, Part 1 – Strategic Planning Overview. Google Images, ed.ac.uk, Strategic Plan 2012-2016. Google Images, cognitivedesignsolutions.com, Planning Process. Google Search, Organizational Planning. Erica Olsen, How to Write a Strategic Plan, page 1.	Page 22
22	Erica Olsen, *How to Write a Strategic Plan*, May 11, 2010, page 1. Available from http://mystrategicplan.com/resources/how-to-write-a-strategic-plan	Page 22
23	David Grusenmeyer, *Mission, Vision, Values & Goals*, page 2. Available from https://www.msu.edu/~steind/estate%20Goals%20Mission%20Values%20Overview_Pro-Dairy%2017pg.pdf	Page 22
24	Ibid, page 35.	Page 22
25	Erica Olsen, *How to Write a Strategic Plan*, May 11, 2010, page 1. Available from http://mystrategicplan.com/resources/how-to-write-a-strategic-plan	Page 23
26	*Mapping a Clear Organization Direction*, Triaxia Partners, Inc., page 4. Available from http://triaxiapartners.com/corp/strategy/articles/Mapping-Clear-Org-Figure	Page 23
27	Ibid, page 3.	Page 23
28	David Grusenmeyer, *Mission, Vision, Values & Goals*, pages 4-5. Available from https://www.msu.edu/~steind/estate%20Goals%20Mission%20Values%20Overview_Pro-Dairy%2017pg.pdf	Page 24

Endnotes

29	Andy Stanley, *Visioneering*, (Colorado Springs, CO: Multnomah Books, 1999). page 12.	Page 24
30	Jim Collins, *Good to Great* (New York: Harper Collins, 2001).	Page 27
31	Greg Coker, *Building Cathedrals – The Power of Purpose* (Chicago Spectrum Press, 2012). (My rendition of this story doesn't exactly match the book *Building Cathedrals* by Greg Coker but is more like I remember it from the sermon I first heard it in.)	Page 32
32	Jim Collins, *Good to Great* (New York: Harper Collins, 2001).	Page 39
33	Zig Ziglar and Tom Ziglar, *Born To Win—Find Your Success Code* (Dallas: SUCCESS Media, 2012), page 3.	Page 62
34	Dan Miller, *Yeah I'm experiencing burnout*, available from http://www.48days.com/yeah-i-confess-im-experiencing-burnout/	Page 63
35	Henry Cloud, Necessary Endings, (New York: Harper Collins, 2010).	Page 63
36	Zig Ziglar and Tom Ziglar, *Born To Win—Find Your Success Code* (Dallas: SUCCESS Media, 2012), page 3.	Page 74

THE POWER OF PURPOSE AND PRIORITIES

Notes

Enjoy additional books by Leon Drennan and Vision Leadership Foundation
Please visit www.vision-leadership.com

You can be a great leader, or a royal pain . . .

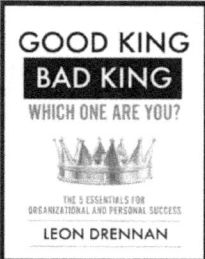

Good King/Bad King captures the essence of excellent leadership and reveals what it takes to live abundantly through five principles of visionary, profitable, and significant leadership. Whether you serve in a for-profit business, a church, nonprofit, or government, the blessing you bring to the people in your care and the organization you lead will make them grateful for your position in their lives. Let Leon Drennan's counsel and guidance show where you are on the path to leading with grace and skill, and inspire your noble pursuit of fine leadership.

Reap while you grow!

LIFE CAN OVERFLOW with the warmth and exuberance of spring or the lavish blessing of a late summer harvest. Other times, the bitter cold of loneliness, loss, or failure leaves you lifeless and desolate. Whatever the season, God can bring a harvest of blessing if you discover what He has for you in each. In *Seasons of the Soul*, Leon Drennan shows how to recognize which season you're experiencing and how to respond to God. If you cooperate with the Master Planner, you can even make the good seasons last longer and the bad seasons end sooner. God will never be one bit harder on you or provide one less miracle than you need. So dig in to this book, and reap a spiritual bounty—whatever your season.

Take a healthy view of the people you lead . . .

. . . AND THE PAIN YOU AVOID MAY BE YOUR OWN. Whether people are a boon or a bother really depends on you. On whether you help them feel like they count. On whether you make it clear where you're leading. And on whether you convince them that going there is what they want, too. You can be a great steward of an organization's resources only if your're a blessing to people. So assimilate the leadership know-how in this book, and establish the right perspective on the people you employ. Because the success of your company, organization, division, or department depends on *you*.

THE POWER OF PURPOSE AND PRIORITIES

www.ingramcontent.com/pod-product-compliance
Lightning Source LLC
Chambersburg PA
CBHW070543300426
44113CB00011B/1771